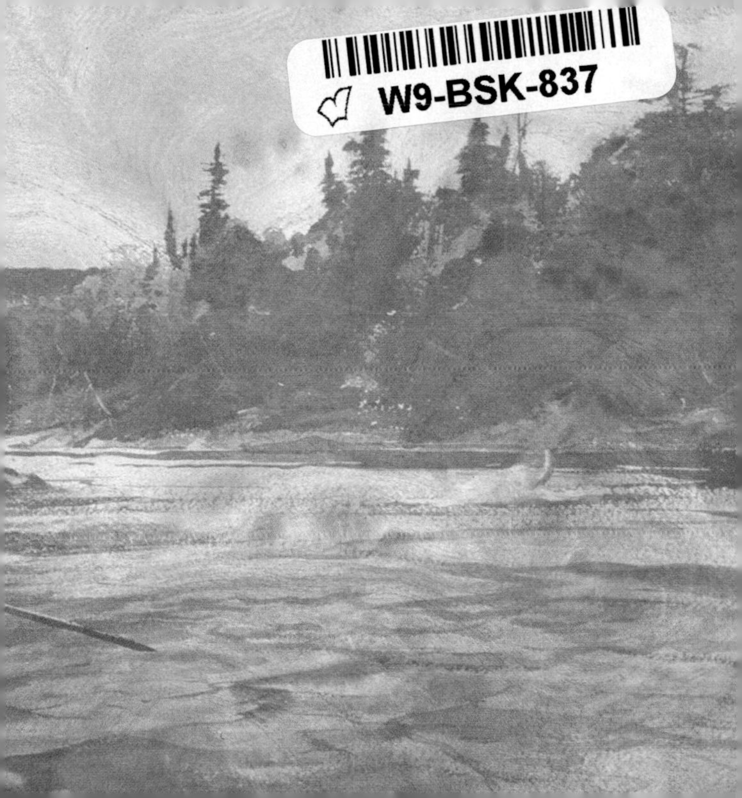

A SPECIAL GIFT

For

....

From

....

Date

....

Illustration Credits

AMERICAN FLY-FISHING MUSEUM
Page 8.

BROWNLOW PRIVATE COLLECTION
Pages 6, 12, 15, 19, 22, 29, 32, 35, 38, 49, 53, 57, 63

WOOD RIVER GALLERY
Pages 25, 45, and cover.

Copyright © 1999
The Brownlow Corporation
6309 Airport Freeway
Fort Worth, Texas. 76117

ISBN: 1-57051-2701

Printed in China

CATCH OF THE DAY

Written and Compiled by
John Paul Brownlow

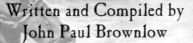

FLY FISHING IN AMERICA

The late nineteenth century was a boom period for fly-fishing and is even regarded by some as the "Golden Age" of the sport. With many fine craftsmen and technological innovations, art and science combined to create beautiful tools for the angler.

Tackle was sold at emerging department stores, some of which specialized in sporting goods. A.G. Spaulding of Chicago, Appleton & Litchfield of Boston, Tryons of Philadelphia, and Abbey & Imbrie of New

York stood out as major tackle retailers of their day.

People learned about angling from books and periodicals. General interest journals like Harper's New Monthly and The Century Magazine periodically published items of interest on fly-fishing, sporting periodicals like Forest & Field included regular segments on fly-fishing, and The American Angler was dedicated entirely to the sport.

And there was plenty to write about. One controversy of the late nineteenth century is of particular interest: the wet vs. dry fly. Some anglers believed that true fly-fishing could only be accomplished if the fly floated on top of the water like a living insect. The debate continues to this day.

THE AMERICAN MUSEUM OF FLY-FISHING

You cannot step twice into the same stream. For as you are stepping in, other and yet other waters flow on.

A faithful man will be richly blessed.

PROVERBS 28:20

Even if it's a little thing, do something
for those who have need of help,
something for which you get
no pay but the privilege
of doing it.

ALBERT SCHWEITZER

President Herbert Hoover, a devoted fisherman.

FISHING

To go fishing is the chance of washing one's soul with pure air, with the rush of the brook, or with the shimmer of the sun on blue water. It brings meekness and inspiration from the decency of nature, charity toward tackle-makers, patience toward fish, a mockery of profits and egos, a quieting of hate, a rejoicing that you do not have to decide anything until next week. And it is discipline in the equality of men—for all men are equal before fish.

HERBERT HOOVER

A PRAYER FOR STRENGTH

I pray to God every night of my life to be given the strength and power to continue my efforts to inspire in others the interest, the obligation and the responsibilities that we owe to this land for the sake of future generations—for my boys and girls—so that we can always look back when the candle of life burns low and say "Thank God I have contributed my best to the land that contributed so much to me."

EDDIE RICKENBACKER

No one knows what game there is in a trout, unless he has fought it out, matching such a rod against a three-pound fish, with forty feet of water underneath, and a clear, unimpeded sweep around him! Ah, then it is that one discovers what will and energy lie within the mottled skin of a trout, and what a miracle of velocity he is when roused.

ADIRONDACK MURRAY

Caught in the Act

Cast all your cares on God;
that anchor holds.

ALFRED, LORD TENNYSON

If a man is truly blessed, he returns
home from fishing to be greeted
by the best catch of his life.

He has achieved success who has lived
well, laughed often, and loved much.

ELBERT HUBBARD

LEARN TO LIVE

Do not live in a hurry. To know how to separate things is to know how to enjoy them. Many finish their fortune sooner than their life; they run through pleasures without enjoying them, and would like to go back when they find they have overleaped their mark.

GRACIA

The man who removes a mountain
begins by carrying away small stones.
ANCIENT PROVERB

When faith is lost, when
honor dies, the man is dead.
JOHN GREENLEAF WHITTIER

To capture the fish is
not all of the fishing.
ZANE GREY

IT LOOKS LIKE COFFEE

Returning from a fishing trip, a man stopped at a roadside diner and ordered a cup of coffee. As he attempted to make conversation with the waitress, he said, "It looks like rain doesn't it?"

She promptly replied, "I can't help what it looks like, we sell it for coffee."

Never buy anything with a
handle on it—it means work.

Clear waters flow from a pure spring.

The secret of life is not to do what one
likes, but to try to like what one has to do.

To his dog, every man is Napoleon; hence
the constant popularity of dogs.

DAILY BLESSINGS

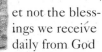 et not the bless-
ings we receive
daily from God
make us not to value or not to praise Him
because they be common; let us not forget
to praise Him for the innocent mirth and
pleasures we have met with since we met
together. What would a blind man give to
see the pleasant rivers and meadows and
flowers and fountains, and this and many
other like blessings we enjoy daily.

IZAAK WALTON
The Complete Angler

Our incomes are like our shoes:
if too small, they pinch, if
too large, we stumble.

COLTON

Better to return and make a net,
than to go down to the stream
and merely wish for fish.

ANCIENT PROVERB

The more I study nature, the more
I am amazed at the Creator.
LOUIS PASTEUR

PACK THE BOAT LIGHT

Let your boat of life be light, packed with only what you need—a homely home and simple pleasures, one or two friends, worth the name, someone to love and someone to love you, a cat, a dog, and enough to wear, and a little more than enough to drink; for thirst is a dangerous thing.

JEROME K. JEROME

ADVENTURES IN THE ADIRONDACKS

In 1869, William H. H. Murray, minister of the Park Street Church in Boston, published *Adventures in the Wilderness; or, Camp-Life in the Adirondacks*. Based on his own experiences, he recounted stories of the mountain air and excellent fishing in upstate New York. His enthusiasm caused many others to flock to the region to battle biting blackflies in search of fish and game.

As a result, Murray came to be known as "Adirondack Murray."

Things do not come neatly labeled "cause" and "effect." We have to decide for ourselves when and where to pin labels.

KEYES

Genius is formed in solitude, character in the stream of human life.

GOETHE

God, you are more majestic than mountains rich with game.

PSALM 76:4

A NEW BEGINNING

Every morning is a fresh beginning. Every day is the world made new. Today is a new day. Today is my world made new. I have lived all my life up to this moment, to come to this day. This moment—this day—is as good as any moment in all eternity. I shall make of this day— a heaven on earth. This is my day of opportunity.

DAN CUSTER

A questioning man is halfway to being wise.
IRISH PROVERB

No person was ever honored for
what he received. Honor has been
the reward for what he gave.
CALVIN COOLIDGE

There are obviously two educations.
One should teach us how to make a
living, and the other how to live.
JAMES T. ADAMS

EVERYDAY TRIUMPHS

The world wants the kind of men who do not shrink from temporary defeats in life; but come again and wrestle triumph from defeat.

THEODORE
ROOSEVELT

NO NEED TO LIE

Oh, give me grace to catch a fish
So big that even I
When talking of it afterwards
May have no need to lie.

ANONYMOUS

We have not inherited the earth
from our fathers, we are borrowing
it from our children.

NATIVE AMERICAN PROVERB

When God measures a man, He puts the
tape around the heart instead of the head.

ANONYMOUS

A smart wife has the pork chops
ready when her husband comes
home from a fishing trip.

ANONYMOUS

GREAT MEN

 There are
no great
men in this world, only great
challenges which ordinary
men rise to meet.

WILLIAM HALSEY, JR.

THE COMPLETE ANGLER

Fishing is an art—or at least it is an art to catch fish.

As for winter fly-fishing— it is as useful as an out of date almanac.

God never made a more calm, quiet, innocent recreation than angling.

Angling may be said to be so like mathematics that it can never be fully learned.

IZZAK WALTON
The Complete Angler, 1653

You must lose a fly to catch a trout.
GEORGE HERBERT

If you wish to know the mind
of a man, listen to his words.
ANCIENT PROVERB

True peace is found by man in
the depths of his own heart,
the dwelling place of God.
JOHANN TAULER

Use what talents you possess. The
woods would be very silent if no birds
sang there except those that sang best.
HENRY VAN DYK

I CAN'T SEE ANYTHING ELSE

A boy was taken by his father on a camping trip in the Adirondacks. They hired a guide, left the beaten trails, and spent a week in the heart of the woods. The boy was greatly impressed by the ability of the guide to see all sorts of things, invisible to the ordinary eye. One day, after the guide had been pointing out some of the hidden secrets of nature, the lad asked with an awed voice, "Mister, can you see God?"

The old man replied, "My boy, it's getting so I can hardly see anything else when I'm out in the woods."

WALTER DUDLEY CAVERT

Heaven seems a little closer in
a house beside the water.
ANONYMOUS

When troubles are few,
dreams are few.
ANCIENT PROVERB

Know the true value of time;
snatch, seize, and enjoy every
moment of it.
LORD CHESTERFIELD

I am not afraid of tomorrow,
for I have seen yesterday
and I love today.
WILLIAM ALLEN WHITE

CHARACTER

Character counts: more than any other factor it determines our reaction to adversity, temptation, sorrow, and approaching death. In every worthwhile aim it determines our success. It limits our influence over others; it decides our destiny; it—and not happiness—is the true end of life. It is the only possession truly our own, the only form of riches immune from the acids of misfortune; the only treasure that cannot corrupt the owner; the only wealth we take with us when we die as capital for a new life's investment.

ANONYMOUS

There is certainly something in angling that tends to produce a gentleness of spirit and a pure serenity of mind.

WASHINGTON IRVING

The brook would lose its song if you removed the rocks.

ANONYMOUS

RULES FOR LIVING

1. Begin each day with a prayer.
2. Work hard.
3. Love your family.
4. Make light of your troubles.
5. Follow the Golden Rule.
6. Read from the Bible.
7. Show kindness.
8. Read worthwhile books.
9. Be clean and pure.
10. Have charity in your heart.
11. Be obedient and respectful.
12. End each day with prayer.

**HANDWRITTEN NOTES
IN A QUAKER BIBLE**

This is the best day the world has ever
seen. Tomorrow will be better.
R. A. CAMPBELL

It is not what we take up, but what
we give up that makes us rich.
HENRY WARD BEECHER

Fear not that thy life shall come
to an end, but rather fear that it
shall never have a beginning.
JOHN HENRY NEWMAN

FISH CAMPS

**D**uring the late nineteenth century, "fish camps," as they were called, became more and more popular. Lake Placid and Saranac Lake in the Adirondacks were two of the most enjoyable destinations.

In 1887, wealthy New York city businessmen founded The North Woods Club. The original objectives of the club were: "boating, fishing, athletic and all manly, lawful sports and pastimes, and the preservation of game and forests."

However, the term "camp" might be misleading as the houses were expensive summer homes built on a grand scale and equipped with all the modern conveniences.

All you need to be a fisherman is patience and a worm.

HERB SHINER

I ASKED GOD

  asked God for
strength that
I might achieve.
I was made weak that I might learn humbly
to obey.
I asked for health that I might do greater things.
I was given infirmity that I might do better things.
I asked for riches that I might be happy.
I was given poverty that I might be wise.
I asked for power that I might have the praise
of men.

I was given weakness that I might feel the
    need of God.
I asked for all things that I might enjoy life.
I was given life that I might enjoy all things.
I got nothing that I asked for, but everything I
had hoped for.

ANONYMOUS

Everything comes
to he who hustles
while he waits.
THOMAS A. EDISON

One machine can
do the work of fifty
ordinary men. No
machine can do
the work of one
extraordinary man.
ELBERT HUBBARD

Life can only be understood backwards; but it must be lived forward.

SOREN KIERKEGAARD

Good will come to him who
is generous and lends freely, who
conducts his affairs with justice.
PSALM 112:5

Men are like trees, each one must put
forth the leaf that is created in him.

If there be any truer measure of a
man than by what he does, it
must be by what he gives.
ROBERT SOUTH

It always was the biggest fish
I caught that got away.
~ EUGENE FIELD

Thinking is the hardest work there
is, which is probably why so
few people engage in it.
HENRY FORD

The wisest man is generally he who
thinks himself the least so.
BOILEAU

A lie is a statement made with intent to deceive. No fisherman makes such statements. When another fisherman asserts that on a certain day and in such a place, he slew so many

IT IS A LIE THAT

trouts, we all know to divide the number and weight by three, half that and knock off ninety percent of the quotient (or whatever it is). And when we retell the story to a third fisherman, we expect him to do likewise. Now such a man may not justly be accused of lying. He does no more than follow a well-recognized and convenient custom.

This instinctive and generous discount which fishermen allow to one another's statements perfectly explains why those statements are so generously conceived.

Enough for Breakfast

FISHERMEN LIE.

It is cruel and wicked and quite unnecessary to assume that they are prompted by any sort of wish to deceive. If I tell another fisherman that I have caught—and I speak the very truth—sixteen trouts weighing.

fifty ounces, he will think I have caught one fish weighing one ounce and risen two others of unknown size. And instead of his admiration, which is my due, I shall earn his contempt, which would be unfair. In order to make him understand precisely what happened, I am compelled to speak in hundreds of fishes and in hundreds of pounds.

Fishermen are simply confirmed and painstaking truthtellers, who all happen to react a little feebly to a certain kind of stimulus.

Now if it's liars you're looking for, don't search the banks of a stream. Go to the golf-links.

WILLIAM CAINE

This world belongs to the man who
is wise enough to change his mind
in the presence of the facts.
ROY L. SMITH

There are no shortcuts to
any place worth going.
ANONYMOUS

There are as good fish in the
sea as ever came out of it.
ENGLISH PROVERB

PROVERBS OF A FISH

Only skilled hands
eat trout.

Even a fish wouldn't
get into trouble if he
kept his mouth shut.

He was a bold man
indeed that first
ate an oyster.

No man can tell whether he is rich
or poor by turning to his ledger. It is
the heart that makes a man rich.

HENRY WARD BEECHER

Blessed is the man who
makes the Lord his trust.

PSALM 40:4

The ability to convert
visions to things is the
secret of success.

HENRY WARD BEECHER

Herbert Hoover, as good a fisherman as he was a president, was equally at home in trout streams and legislative assemblies. Responding to each arena of life he said:

All men are equal before fish.

Peace is not made at the council table, or by treaties, but in the hearts of men.

ONE DAY AT A TIME

No man ever sank beneath the burden of the day. It is when tomorrow's burden is added to the burden of today that the weight is more than we can bear. It is delightfully easy to live one day at a time.

GEORGE MacDONALD

The only things worth
learning are the things you
know after you know it all.
HARRY S. TRUMAN

Everybody should have a dream.
JESSE OWENS

Many men owe the grandeur of their
lives to their tremendous difficulties.
CHARLES H. SPURGEON

IT TAKES
FEW WORDS
TO TELL
THE TRUTH.

CHIEF JOSEPH
OF THE NEZ PERCÉ

It does not take great men to do great
things; it only takes consecrated men.
PHILLIPS BROOKS

When I have learnt to love God
better than my earthly dearest, I shall love my earthly
dearest better than I do now.
C. S. LEWIS

Pray not for lighter burdens
but for stronger backs.
THEODORE ROOSEVELT